HILARIOUS JOKES

FOR

YEAR OLD KIDS

A Message From the Publisher

Hello! My name is Hayden and I am the owner of Hayden Fox Publishing, the publishing house that brought you this title.

My hope is that you and your young comedian love this book and enjoy every single page. If you do, please think about **giving us your honest feedback via a review on Amazon**. It may only take a moment, but it really does mean the world for small businesses like mine.

Even if you happen to not like this title, please let us know the reason in your review so that we may improve this title for the future and serve you better.

The mission of Hayden Fox is to create premium content for children that will help them increase their confidence and grow their imaginations while having tons of fun along the way.

Without you, however, this would not be possible, so we sincerely thank you for your purchase and for supporting our company mission.

Sincerely,
Hayden Fox

What's a fatigued pea called?

Sleep-pea

What do you call two guys hanging on the window?

Kurt and Rod

--= DID YOU KNOW? =--

The first 4th of July celebration was in 1777 during the middle of the Revolutionary War.

 The opposite sides of the dice always add up to seven.

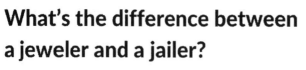

What's the difference between a jeweler and a jailer?

RIDDLES

One sells watches while another watches cells.

What's something that happens twice in a moment, once a minute, but never in one thousand years?

The letter "M"

Coy knows pseudonoise codes.

TONGUE TWISTER

Knock Knock!

Who's there?

Celeste.

Celeste who?

Celeste time I'm going to tell this joke!

Why was the computer so tired when it got home?

Because it had a hard drive!

How do construction workers celebrate?

They raise the roof!

DID YOU KNOW?

You might think that stars all look the same, but each star is a different colour depending on their temperature.

**Six sticky skeletons,
six sticky skeletons,
six sticky skeletons...**

TONGUE TWISTER

RIDDLES

My pockets are empty, yet they still have something in them. How?

They have a hole in them.

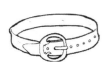

The belt was arrested. Why is this?

It was holding up the pants hostage.

DID YOU KNOW?

Earth is estimated to be about 4.5 billion years old!

 **Where do college aged vampires like to shop?**

Forever 21

What did the asparagus say to the mushroom?

You're a fun-gi!

 **Knock Knock!**

Who's there?
Wooden shoe.
Wooden shoe who?
Wooden shoe like to hear another joke?

With dinner, an invisible man enjoys drinking what?

Evaporated milk.

Despite wanting to play a game of cards, the sailor couldn't. Why is this?'

The captain was standing on the deck.

What do you call a snake on a building site?

A boa constructor.

Who's there?

Cugat.

Cugat who?

Cugat to love my jokes!

Knock Knock!

Why did the dinosaur refuse to wear deodorant?

He didn't want to be ex-stink.

What do you call a belt with a clock on it?

A waist of time.

☰ DID YOU KNOW? ☰

It is not possible to walk on gaseous planets like Jupiter, Neptune, and Uranus since they don't have a solid surface to walk on.

Who's there?
Darby.
Darby who?
Darby a lot of reasons why I knocked.

Knock Knock!

Plymouth sleuths thwart Luther's slithering.

TONGUE TWISTER

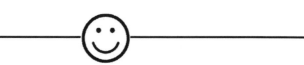

How do you pay for parking in space?

A parking meteor.

What do you call two giraffes colliding?

A giraffe-ic jam.

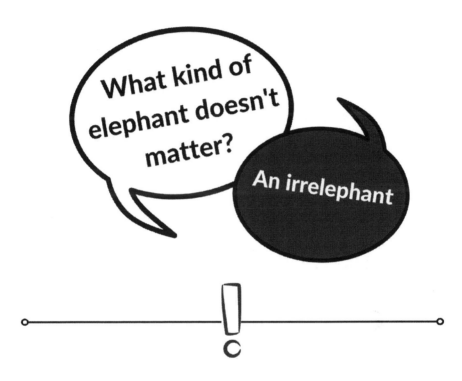

What kind of elephant doesn't matter?

An irrelephant

⚡ DID YOU KNOW? ⚡

The world's heaviest carrot grown by Christopher Qualley in the USA weighed 10.7kg (or 22.44 lb).

If a bull charges you, what's the best thing to do?

Pay the bull what you owe.

When an outlaw stole a calendar, what did he end up getting?

Twelve months.

Rory the warrior and Roger the worrier in a rural brewery.

TONGUE TWISTER

Knock Knock!

Who's there?
Dismay.
Dismay who?
Dismay be one of my worst ones yet!

 **What do you call a ghost's mom and dad?**

Transparents

Why did the can crusher quit his job?

Because it was soda pressing.

⟶ DID YOU KNOW? ⟵

 **Ham the Astrochimp was the first hominid in space, launched on Jan. 31, 1961.**

A neutron star can spin 600 times ★ in one second.

What do you call an ant that won't go away?

Perman-ant

What does a nosey pepper do?

Gets jalapeño business.

Who's there?

Genoa.

Genoa who?

Genoa any new knock-knock jokes?

Knock Knock!

Who's there?

Amish.

Amish who?

Really? You don't look like a shoe!

Knock Knock!

What kind of cheese is made backward?

RIDDLES

Edam.

I hated my job as an origami teacher...

Too much paperwork.

DID YOU KNOW?

The very first animals in space were fruit flies...they were sent up in 1947 and recovered alive.

Europa, one of Jupiter's moons, has saltwater geysers that are 20x taller than Mt. Everest.

How do you make gold soup?

Put in 14 carrots.

Really leery, rarely Larry.

Knock Knock!

Who's there?
Nana.
Nana who?
Nana your business!

Six Czech cricket critics.

Knock Knock!

Who's there?
Elly.
Elly who?
Elly-mentary, my dear Watson!

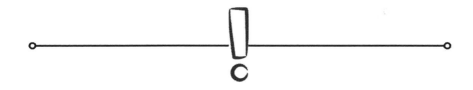

DID YOU KNOW?

Alpha Centauri isn't a star, but a star system. It is 4.22 light years away.

Which kind of ship has two mates but no captain?

Relationship.

What can fill a room but takes up no space?

Light.

What do you call a wizard that comes from space?

A flying sorcerer!

What is a math teacher's favourite dessert?

Pi!

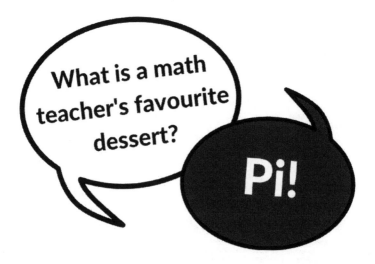

Why did the Cyclops close his school?

Because he only had one pupil.

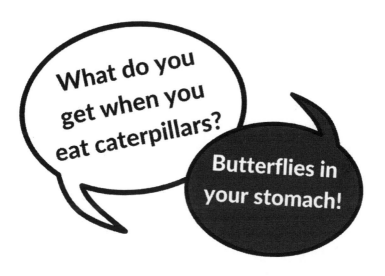

What do you get when you eat caterpillars?

Butterflies in your stomach!

What does the sun skate on?

Solarblades!

DID YOU KNOW?

Moose are born knowing how to swim. An adult moose can swim up to 6 miles per hour and maintain that pace for 2 hours.

A man calls his dog from the opposite side of the river. The dog crosses the river without getting wet, and without using a bridge or boat. How?

The river is frozen.

An electric train is traveling south so which way is the smoke blowing?

There is no smoke; it's an electric train.

Pail of ale aiding ailing Al's travails.

TONGUE TWISTER

Octopus ocular optics.

Who's there?

Maida.

Maida who?

Maida force be with you!

Knock Knock!

Do skunks celebrate Valentine's Day?

Yes, they're very scent-imental!

What sounds does a space turkey make?

Hubble, hubble, hubble.

-- DID YOU KNOW? --

Your mouth makes 25,000 gallons of saliva in a lifetime. All that spit could fill two Olympic swimming pools!

What is black when it's first purchased, red while being used, and grey when it's thrown away?

Charcoal.

Why did the person wear a helmet to the dinner table?

Because they were on a "crash diet."

East Fife Four, Forfar Five  TONGUE TWISTER

 Knock Knock!

Who's there?

Padmé.

Padmé who?

Padmé to open the door.
I'm the locksmith.

What do you call a pig that gets fired from his job?

Canned ham!

Why did the apple go out with the prune?

She couldn't find a date.

Who's there?
Tennis.
Tennis who?
Tennis five plus five.

Who's there?
Wevilly.
Wevilly who?
Wevilly want to come in please!

--- **DID YOU KNOW?** ---

 Some starfish can regenerate a new body from a single severed arm.

You can't sneeze in your sleep because the **brain shuts down the reflex.**

Scissors sizzle, thistles sizzle.

 *TONGUE TWISTER*

Knock Knock!

Who's there?
To.
To who?
It's to whom.

What does a thesaurus eat for dessert?

A synonym roll.

DID YOU KNOW?

Jumping rope is one of the best forms  of cardio you can do. It burns 500-1000 calories per hour!

Cooks cook cupcakes quickly, cooks cook cupcakes quickly, cooks cook cupcakes quickly...

TONGUE TWISTER

Knock Knock!

Who's there?

Ailene.

Ailene who?

Ailened on the door and it opened.

 **I bought the world's worst thesaurus...**

Not only is it terrible, it's also terrible.

DID YOU KNOW?

Snakes can burp fire—only if the decomposing animal they eat bursts with methane and hydrogen while being digested.

A happy hippo hopped and hiccupped.

TONGUE TWISTER

Who's there?
Spell.
Spell who?
Okay, w-h-o.

What do you call an ant who fights crime?

A vigilantly!

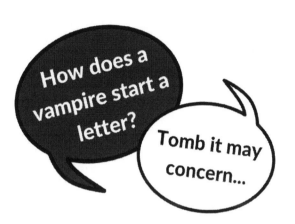

How does the moon cut his hair?

Eclipse it.

Who's there?

Czech.

Czech who?

Czech before you open the door!

DID YOU KNOW?

In 1773, after the Boston Tea Party, it was considered to be "patriotic duty" to switch from drinking tea to drinking coffee.

Green glass globes glow greenly.

TONGUE TWISTER

Knock Knock!

Who's there?

Alpaca.

Alpaca who?

Alpaca the suitcase, you load the car!

What do you call a droid that takes the long way around?

R2 detour.

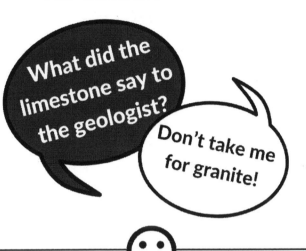

What did the limestone say to the geologist?

Don't take me for granite!

Who's there?
Isaiah.
Isaiah who?
Isaiah nothing till you open this door!

Who's there?
Theodore.
Theodore who?
Theodore is stuck and it won't open!

⚪ DID YOU KNOW? ⚪

The world's oldest known bird is a Layman Albatross named Wisdom.
As of 2021, she is 71 years old.

Eleven benevolent elephants, eleven benevolent elephants, eleven benevolent elephants...

TONGUE TWISTER

Knock Knock!

Who's there?
Cargo.
Cargo who?
No, car go BEEP BEEP!

Why couldn't the 11yr old get into the pirate movie?

Because it was rated ARRRRRRR!

Why did the dinosaur cross the road?

Because the chicken wasn't born yet.

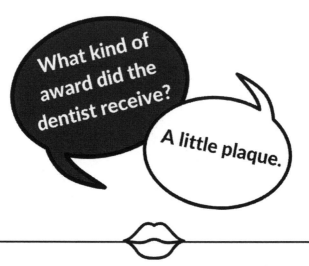

What kind of award did the dentist receive?

A little plaque.

A snake sneaks to seek a snack.

Who's there?

Europe.

Europe who?

No, YOU're a poo!

Why are ghosts bad liars?

Because you can see right through them.

Why did the invisible man turn down the job offer?

Because he couldn't see himself doing it.

DID YOU KNOW?

The largest tree in the world—the giant sequoia, also known as General Sherman—measures up to 52,508 cubic feet.

According to the United Nations, by 2025, 2/3 of the world's population is going to face water scarcity.

A pessimistic pest exists amidst us.

TONGUE TWISTER

Knock Knock!

Who's there?

Irene.

Irene who?

Irene and Irene but still no one answers the door!

What did the astronaut say when he crashed into the moon?

"I Apollo-gize."

What dinosaur had the best vocabulary?

The thesaurus.

What did one DNA strand say to the other DNA strand?

Do these genes look ok?

Why aren't dogs good dancers?

They have two left feet.

Six sleek swans swam swiftly southwards.

TONGUE TWISTER

Knock Knock!

Who's there?
Isabelle.
Isabelle who?
Isabelle necessary on the door?

What did one toilet say to the other?

You look flushed.

What happened when the skunk was on trial?

The judge declared, "Odor in the court, odor in the court!"

⟜ DID YOU KNOW? ⟜

Despite the colossal size of the project, the designing, planning, and construction of The Empire State Building only took 20 months.

Imagine an imaginary menagerie manager managing an imaginary menagerie.

Who's there?
Abyssinia.
Abyssinia, who?
Abyssinia soon.

What do you think of that new diner on the moon?

Food was good, but there really wasn't much atmosphere.

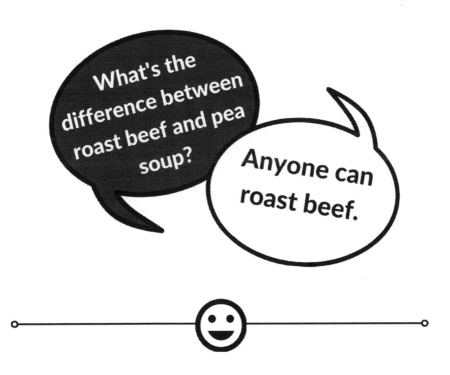

What's the difference between roast beef and pea soup?

Anyone can roast beef.

Who's there?

Knock Knock!

Augusta.

Augusta who?

Augusta go home now!

DID YOU KNOW?

It is possible to play rugby underwater.
It's literally called "underwater rugby".

She sells seashells by the seashore of Seychelles.

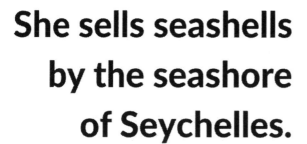

Knock Knock!

Who's there?
Botany.
Botany who?
Botany good locks lately?

Why didn't the koala bear get the job?

They said she was over-koala-fied.

What did the lunchbox say to the banana?

You really have appeal.

Who's there?
Avenue.
Knock Knock!
Avenue who?
Avenue knocked on this door before?

Who's there?
Germany.
Knock Knock!
Germany who?
Germany people knocking on your door today?

⚡ DID YOU KNOW? ⚡

Peacocks are male while peahens are female.

Bertrand Bookstore in Lisbon, Portugal is the oldest bookstore in the world. It opened in 1732.

Knock Knock!

Who's there?
Big interrupting cow.
Big interrupting cow wh-?
MOOOOOOO!

To begin to toboggan
first buy a toboggan,
but don't buy
too big a toboggan.

TONGUE TWISTER

Why did Humpty Dumpty have a great fall?

To make up for his miserable summer.

Why did the woman become an archeologist?

Because her career was in ruins.

Who's there?
Thor.
Thor who?
Thor knuckleth from knocking!

Knock Knock!

Who's there?
Iguana.
Iguana who?
Iguana come inside.

Knock Knock!

⚡ DID YOU KNOW? ⚡

Chickens are the closest living relatives to the T-Rex.

☺

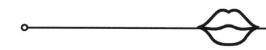

Who's there?

Wiccan.

Wiccan who?

Wiccan make beautiful music together!

If a dog chews shoes,  **whose shoes does he choose?**

What do you call two monkeys that share an Amazon account?

Primemates!

What do you call babies in the army?

Infantry!

⚡ DID YOU KNOW? ⚡

The unicorn is the national animal of Scotland. This is because of its association with chivalry, purity, and innocence in Celtic mythology.

Knock Knock!

Who's there?

Cynthia.

Cynthia who?

Cynthia been away, I missed you.

How many boards
Could the Mongols hoard
If the Mongol hoards
got bored?

TONGUE TWISTER

What would happen if the dean lost his job?

He would lose his "ideanity".

Why did the scarecrow win an award?

Because he was out standing in his field.

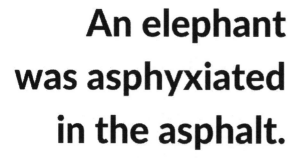

Who's there?
Theresa.
Theresa who?
Theresa nothing like a good good knock knock joke!

Who's there?
Tyson.
Tyson who?
Tyson garlic around your neck to ward off vampires!

An elephant was asphyxiated in the asphalt.

Why did the scientist take out the bell?

He wanted to win the no-bell prize.

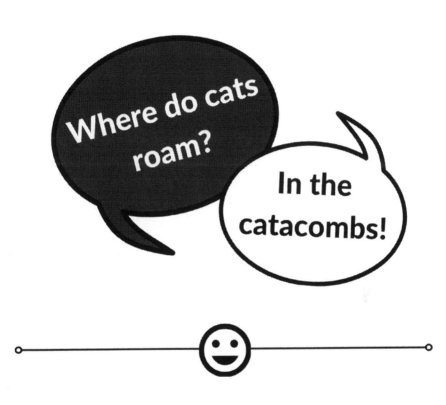

Where do cats roam?

In the catacombs!

Who's there?

Vitamin.

Vitamin who?

Vitamin for a party!

Knock Knock!

Knock Knock!

Who's there?
Acid!
Acid who?
Acid down and be quiet!

Knock Knock!

Who's there?
A little old lady.
A little old lady who?
I didn't know you could yodel!

How much myrtle would a wood turtle hurdle if a wood turtle could hurdle myrtle?

TONGUE TWISTER

What do you call a bear in the rain?

A drizzly bear.

What do Olympic sprinters eat before a race?

Nothing. They fast.

Who's there?
Stopwatch.
Stopwatch who?
Stopwatch you're
doing and let me in!

Who's there?
Leslie.
Leslie who?
Leslie town and go
camping.

**Knock
Knock!**

**Knock
Knock!**

There was a minimum
of cinnamon in the
aluminum pan.

 **How much does a pirate pay for corn?**

A BUCK-aneer.

Who's there?

Yvette.

Yvette who?

Yvette helps a lot of animals!

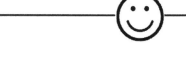

Why aren't koalas actual bears?

They don't meet the koalafications.

What do you get when you cross a poodle, a cocker spaniel and a rooster?

A cocker-poodle-doo

What's a king's favorite kind of weather?

Reign.

Who's there?
Yah.
Yah who?
No, I prefer google.

Why do melons have to have a wedding ceremony?

Because they cantaloupe!

Yellow butter, purple jelly, red jam, black bread. Spread it thick, say it quick!

What happened with the kidnapping situation in the park?

They woke him up.

Who's there?

Panther.

Panther who?

Panther no panth I'm going thwimming.

Knock Knock!

RIDDLES

I have lakes with no water, mountains with no stone and cities with no buildings. What am I?

A map.

If eleven plus two equals one, what does nine plus five equal?

11 o'clock plus 2 hours = 1 o'clock
9 o'clock plus 5 hours = 2 o'clock

Richard's wretched ratchet wrench.

TONGUE TWISTER

Why did the actor fall through the floorboards?

He was just going through a stage.

What do you call a parade of rabbits hopping backward?

A receding hare-line.

?

RIDDLES

What English word retains the same pronunciation, even after you take away four of its five letters?

Queue.

What's red and smells like blue paint?

Red paint.

Knock Knock!

Who's there?
Closure.
Closure who?
Closure mouth when you're eating!

The thirty-three thieves thought that they thrilled the throne throughout Thursday.

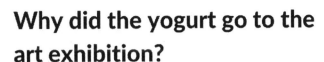

Why did the yogurt go to the art exhibition?

Because it was cultured.

What do piggies use when they have an infection?

Antibiotic oinkment.

?

What can go up a chimney when down but cannot go down a chimney when up?

RIDDLES

An umbrella.

George, Helen, and Steve are drinking coffee. Bert, Karen, and Dave are drinking soda. Using logic, is Elizabeth drinking coffee or soda?

Coffee. The letter E appears twice in her name, as it does in the names of the others drinking coffee.

Who's there?

Justin.

Justin who?

Justin the neighborhood
and thought I'd come over!

Who's there?

Henrietta.

Henrietta who?

Henrietta worm that
was in his apple.

Knock Knock!

Knock Knock!

**There was a fisherman
named Fisher who fished
for some fish in a fissure.**

TONGUE TWISTER

Did you hear about the cheese factory that exploded in France?

There was nothing left but de Brie.

What do you get from a pampered cow?

Spoiled milk.

?

What is set on a table, cut, and then never eaten?

A deck of cards.

RIDDLES

One night, a butcher, baker, and candlestick maker go to a hotel. However, when they get their bill, it's for four people. Who's the fourth person?

The night (knight) makes four people!

What did the snail say when riding on the turtle's back?

Wheeeeeee!

Who's there?

Pasta.

Pasta who?

Pasta la vista, baby.

A really leery Larry rolls readily to the road.

Lucky rabbits like to cause a ruckus.

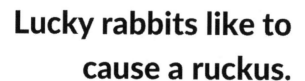

Why were they called the Dark Ages?

Because there were lots of knights.

Why do gorillas have big nostrils?

Because they have big fingers!

What has a head, a tail, is brown, and has no legs?

RIDDLES

A penny.

It lives with no body, hears with no ears, speaks with no mouth, and is born in air. What is it?

An echo.

It can be served up, but no one ever takes a bite out of it. What is it?

A tennis ball.

I am four times as old as my daughter. In 20 years time I shall be twice as old as her. How old are we now?

I am 40 and my daughter is 10.

Red Buick, blue Buick, Red Buick, blue Buick, Red Buick, blue Buick...

TONGUE TWISTER

Who's there?

Plato.

Plato who?

Plato fish and chips, please.

-- **Knock Knock!** --

Why don't ants ever get sick?

Because they have little anty bodies.

What's the best thing about Switzerland?

I don't know, but the flag is a big plus.

You are given three positive numbers that can be added and multiplied, yet the results remain the same. What are these numbers?

1, 2, and 3.

What common English verb becomes its own past tense by rearranging its letters?

Eat and ate.

Who's there?
Esme.
Esme who?
Esme tea ready yet?

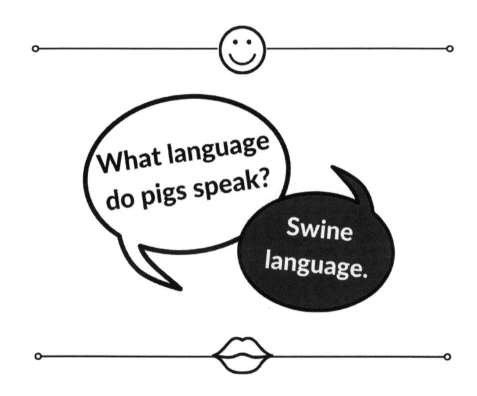

What language do pigs speak?

Swine language.

**If you notice this notice,
you will notice
that this notice
is not worth noticing.**

TONGUE TWISTER

Which rock group has four guys who can't sing or play instruments?

Mount Rushmore.

Why did the A go to the bathroom and come out as an E?

Because he had a vowel movement.

☀ DID YOU KNOW? ☀

 Cashews come from a fruit.

Most elephants weigh less than a blue whale's tongue!

 From the time Pluto was discovered until the time it was demoted from planethood, it still hadn't made one complete revolution around the Sun.

RIDDLES

You see a boat full of people yet there is not a single person on board. How is this possible?

All of those onboard are married.

You walk into a dark room holding a match and find a kerosene lamp, a candle, and a fireplace. Which do you light first?

The match.

Knock Knock!

Who's there?
Quentin.
Quentin who?
Quentin my thirst!

Which wristwatches are Swiss wristwatches?

TONGUE TWISTER

DID YOU KNOW?

The Romans were some of the first people to wear bikinis.

 In Japan, more paper is used to make manga than toilet paper.

The measurement of time, the second, is called that because it's the second division of the hour.

Crows have accents depending on the region they come from/grew up.

Who's there?
Raichu
Raichu who?
Raichu are!

What did the pirate say on his 80th birthday?

Ayyee Matey!

Peter Piper picked a peck of pickled peppers.

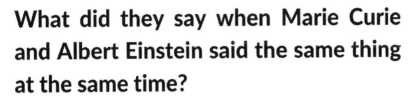

What did they say when Marie Curie and Albert Einstein said the same thing at the same time?

Greatest minds think alike!

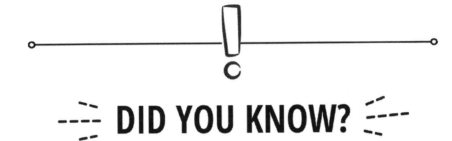

DID YOU KNOW?

Yoda and Miss Piggy were both voiced by the same person.

The word oxymoron is actually an oxymoron in itself. The root oxy meaning sharp. While the root moron meaning dull. That's also where the word moron comes from.

Knock Knock!

Who's there?

Dishes.

Dishes who?

Dishes the police! Open up!

Who's there?

Ivan

Ivan who?

Ivan. You lose!

Knock Knock!

Who's there?

Goliath

Goliath who?

Goliath down you're looking tired.

Knock Knock!

I thought a thought.
But the thought I thought
Wasn't the thought I
thought I thought.

TONGUE TWISTER

Why did the God of Thunder need to stretch his muscles so much as a kid?

He was always a little Thor.

I have no blood pumping through me, but I have four fingers and one thumb. What am I?

A glove.

It's shorter than the rest but when you're happy you raise it up like it's the best. What is it?

A thumb.

Tim, the thin twin tinsmith.

Who's there?
Jamaica
Jamaica who?
Jamaica great keyboard player!

Knock Knock!

Who's there?
Zaire
Zaire who?
Zaire is polluted!

Knock Knock!

There's a sandwich on the sand which was sent by a sane witch.

TONGUE TWISTER

When fish are in schools...

they sometimes take debate.

What happened with the kidnapping situation in the park?

They woke him up.

What's the difference between people from Dubai and people from Abu Dhabi?

People from Dubai don't watch the Flintstones...
People from ABUUUU DHABBBIIIII DOOOOOO!

Why do seagulls fly over the sea?

Because if they flew over the bay, they'd be bagels!

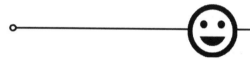

Knock Knock!

Who's there?
Impatient cow.
Impatient cow wh-?
Mooooo!

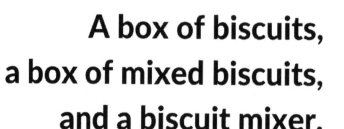

A box of biscuits, a box of mixed biscuits, and a biscuit mixer.

TONGUE TWISTER

What kind of nut does not have a shell?

A doughnut

Why did the shrimp refuse to share her treasure?

She was being a little shellfish!

?

What do you call a person who doesn't have all of their fingers on one hand?

RIDDLES

Normal because all fingers should be on two hands, not one.

Which room is one without doors or windows?

Mushroom.

Knock Knock!

Who's there?
Cereal
Cereal who?
Cereal pleasure to meet you!

Knock Knock!

Who's there?
Leonie.
Leonie who?
Leonie one I tell knock-knock jokes to is you.

Thirty-three thousand feathers on a thrushes throat.

TONGUE TWISTER

The difference between broccoli and boogers?

Kids don't eat broccoli!

What starts with "P," ends with "E," and contains hundreds of letters inside?

Post Office

What do an island and the letter "T" have in common?

They are both in the middle of "water."

DID YOU KNOW?

Walt Disney said silent film star Charlie Chaplin was an inspiration for Mickey Mouse.

Knock Knock!

Who's there?

Who.

Who who?

What is this, Harry Potter's Sanctuary for Injured Owls?

Knock Knock!

Who's there?

Mavis!

Mavis who?

Mavis be the last time I knock on this door!

If practice makes perfect and perfect needs practice, I'm perfectly practiced and practically perfect.

TONGUE TWISTER

Where do crayons go on holiday?

Color-ado

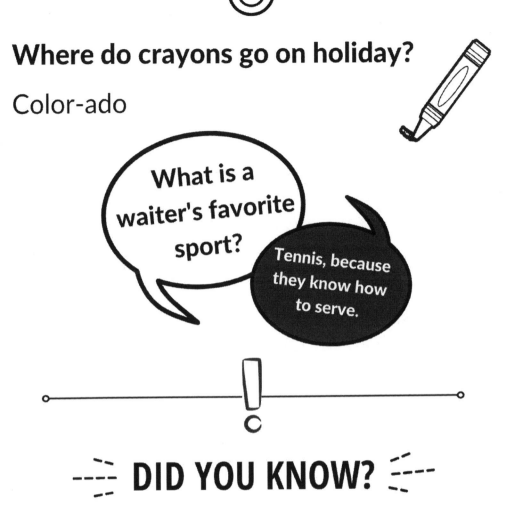

What is a waiter's favorite sport?

Tennis, because they know how to serve.

DID YOU KNOW?

1.7% of the world's water is frozen (the fresh water is trapped in glaciers) and unfortunately, unusable.

The reason Kansas and Arkansas are pronounced differently is because Kansas is an English word while Arkansas is a French word.

Near an ear, a nearer ear,
a nearly eerie ear

I like New York, unique New York, I like unique New York.

Knock Knock!

Who's there?

Bjorn.

Bjorn who?

Bjorn on the fourth of July.

DID YOU KNOW?

Canada has more lakes than the rest of the world combined.

Roughly 7% of all humans who have ever lived are still alive today.

What school do planets and stars go to to study?

UNIVERSity!

Where do dogs go when they lose their tail?

To the retail store.

--- DID YOU KNOW? ---

In The Wizard of Oz, the snow in the poppy scene was made of asbestos.

There are health benefits to popcorn, including help build bone, muscle and tissues, and aids digestion.

--⋮ DID YOU KNOW? ⋮--

In terms of astrology, most people have aspects of every 12 signs in their chart.

Knock Knock!

Who's there?
Mayflower.
Mayflower who?
Mayflowers bloom by Plymouth rock.

Knock Knock!

Who's there?
Adair.
Adair who?
Adair you to do it again!

What do you call two spiders who got married?

Newlyweb!

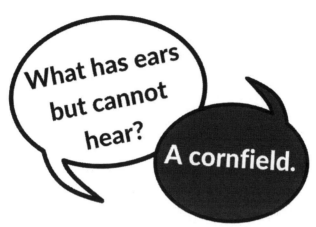

What has ears but cannot hear?

A cornfield.

Why was the computer cold?

It had a virus.

DID YOU KNOW?

A group of frogs is called an army.

 Monkeys can go bald in old age, just like humans.

He freely threw three free throws

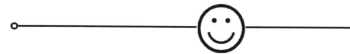

How many tickles does it take to make an octopus laugh?

10 tickles!

Who's there?
De Niro.
De Niro who?
De Niro I get to you, the happier I am!

Why are robots never afraid?

They have nerves of steel.

What does bread do on vacation?

Loaf around.

-⫶- DID YOU KNOW? ⫶--

 The biggest pizza ever created was 13,580 square feet, made in Rome, Italy.

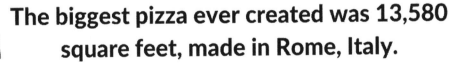 **The artists who voiced Mickey Mouse & Minnie Mouse were married in real life.**

A synonym for cinnamon is a cinnamon synonym.

TONGUE TWISTER

Knock Knock!

Who's there?
Doctor.
Doctor who?
That's one of my favourite shows!

Knock Knock!

Who's there?
Olive!
Olive who?
Olive you!

Why did the giraffes get bad grades?

She had her head in the clouds.

What is a scarecrow's favorite fruit?

A strawberry.

?

A monkey, a squirrel, and a bird are racing to the top of a coconut tree. Who will get the banana first?

None of them because a banana can't grow from a coconut tree.

RIDDLES

A man in a car saw a Golden Door, Silver Door, and a Bronze Door. Which door did he open first?

The car door.

Where does Superman's wife drive?

Lois' lane.

How did the baby tell her mom she had a wet diaper?

She sent her a pee-mail.

Who's there?

Butcher.

Butcher who?

Butcher eggs all in one basket.

Knock Knock!

Who's there?

Pierre.

Pierre who?

Pierre through the keyhole, you'll see.

Knock Knock!

Why did the garden feel overcrowded?

There wasn't mushroom.

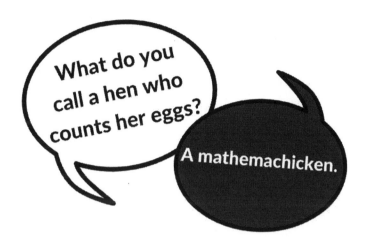

What do you call a hen who counts her eggs?

A mathemachicken.

Why did Mom hit the cake with a hammer?

It was a pound cake.

Any noise annoys an oyster but a noisy noise annoys an oyster more.

TONGUE TWISTER

Fred fed Ted bread and Ted fed Fred bread.

What can never be put in a saucepan?

Its lid.

When asked how old she was, Suzie replied, "In two years I will be twice as old as I was five years ago." How old is she?

She's 12.

What do you say when you catch a ghost?

"Gotchu Boo!"

Which bird has the worst manners?

Mocking birds.

What kind of dog does Dracula have?

A bloodhound!

DID YOU KNOW?

A group of butterflies is called a kaleidoscope.

Wooly mammoths were still around when the Pyramids were being built.

Each Easter Eddie eats eighty Easter eggs.

TONGUE TWISTER

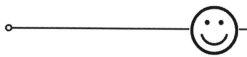
Knock Knock!

Who's there?
Cannelloni.
Cannelloni who?
Cannelloni some money till next week?

What's the difference between a rabbit at the gym and a rabbit with a carrot up its nose?

One's a fit bunny, the other's a bit funny.

What sort of appliance does a monkey use?

A gorilla. (A griller)

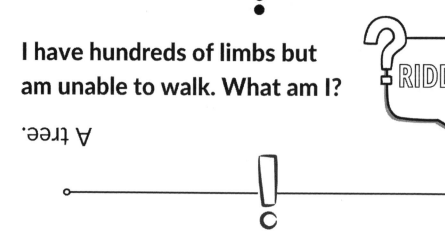

I have hundreds of limbs but am unable to walk. What am I?

RIDDLES

A tree.

⫶ DID YOU KNOW? ⫶

'Arachibutyrophobia' is the fear of getting peanut butter stuck to the roof of your mouth.

Popular musicians' lifespan are 25 years shorter than the general population.

Knock Knock!

Who's there?
Radio.
Radio who?
Radio or not here I come!

How do you make a strawberry shake?

Tell it a scary story!

What is worse than raining cats and dogs?

Hailing taxis!

 **DID YOU KNOW?**

In France, a "crepe" is just a really thin pancake.

 Alpacas are known to spit when they get annoyed.

Who's there?

Ana.

Ana who?

Another mosquito.

Who's there?

Buddha.

Buddha who?

Buddha this slice of bread for me!

DID YOU KNOW?

We know more about the surface of the moon than we do the ocean floor.

The only 15 letter word that can be spelled without repeating a letter is uncopyrightable.

Leave Your Feedback on Amazon

Please think about leaving some feedback via a review on Amazon. It may only take a moment, but it really does mean the world for small businesses like mine.

Even if you did not enjoy this title, please let us know the reason(s) in your review so that we may improve this title and serve you better.

From the Publisher

Hayden Fox's mission is to create premium content for children that will help them expand their vocabulary, grow their imaginations, gain confidence, and share tons of laughs along the way.

Without you, however, this would not be possible, so we sincerely thank you for your purchase and for supporting our company mission.

Thank you for reading!

Manufactured by Amazon.ca
Bolton, ON

20794782R00059